For Reading
Out Loud

For Reading Out Loud

PLANNING AND PRACTICE

Bobbi Fisher

and

Emily Fisher Medvic

Foreword by Jim Trelease

HEINEMANN
Portsmouth, NH

KH

Heinemann
A division of Reed Elsevier Inc.
361 Hanover Street
Portsmouth, NH 03801–3912
www.heinemann.com

Offices and agents throughout the world

Library of Congress Cataloging-in-Publication Data
Fisher, Bobbi.
    For reading out loud : planning and practice / Bobbi Fisher, Emily Fisher Medvic ; foreword by Jim Trelease.
        p. cm.
    Includes bibliographical references.
    ISBN 0-325-00436-6 (alk. paper)
    1. Oral reading. 2. Children—Books and reading. I. Medvic, Emily Fisher.
II. Title.

    LB1573.5 .F57 2003
    372.45'2—dc21

                                                                    2002014977

Editor: Lois Bridges
Production: Vicki Kasabian
Cover design: Jenny Jensen Greenleaf
Cover illustration: Lynn Jeffery
Typesetter: Tom Allen, Pear Graphic Design
Manufacturing: Steve Bernier

Printed in the United States of America on acid-free paper
07 06 05   VP   3 4 5

8/28/09

For Colin, Jemma, Clement, and Abigail

Contents

Foreword

When Joseph LeDoux was a butcher's son growing up in Louisiana, his father often asked him to help by cleaning the membranes off the cow brains, along with extracting the occasional bullet (that was how the steers were killed in those days). Today LeDoux is one of America's most renowned neuroscientists, specializing in brain research—humans' this time.

When Wernher von Braun was a child growing up in Germany, it was the custom for parents to give their child his first pair of long pants when he was confirmed. Not Wernher's parents. He received his first telescope upon being confirmed, the precursor of a life that would be spent focused on the stars and establishing America's space program.

These are but two examples among scores that offer solid evidence that the writer David Kherdian was right when he wrote: "What we learn in childhood is carved in stone; what we learn as adults is carved in ice." That's why we as adults find it easier to remember the name of our elementary school classmates or our grandmother's telephone number than to recall the names of the couple we met at a party last weekend. Childhood experiences always loom larger and stay longer.

And all of that is why reading aloud to children—and this book—is so important. Almost twenty years ago, the U.S. Department of Education's Commission on Reading concluded that reading aloud to children is "the single most important activity for building the knowledge required for eventual success in reading." Nothing has changed in the last twenty years to make it any less important, though a few things have made it more difficult. Most of those things have to do with certain people who are fixated with testing and score keeping, number crunchers who think they can make the same demands of students and teachers that they make of the poor scriveners in their accounting departments.

So now anything and everything done in the classroom must be justified. How do those ten minutes of story time dovetail with the state's new standards for first grade? Fortunately, they can be justified. To begin with, listening comprehension comes before reading comprehension. If you've never heard the word *enormous*, it's unlikely you'll ever say it. And if you've neither heard it nor said it, imagine how difficult it'll be to read and write it.

That listening vocabulary (which feeds the speaking, reading, and writing vocabularies) proves most critical in the first four years of school when nearly all the instruction is oral. Thus the child with the most words in his or her head understands the most of what the teacher is teaching. So when research shows at-risk students enter kindergarten having heard 32 million words fewer than their advantaged classmates, there is a crying need for someone to fill their listening vocabularies in the classroom. It is all the more critical if those same children come from homes where there is a dearth of printed material (which contains the richest of vocabularies).

But there is something in this reading aloud that is even greater than vocabulary development. It is an area that is largely ignored in the testing mania: Motivation. How ironic that such a substance is so totally ignored in federal mandates yet it feeds some of the greatest success stories in business and politics.

Motivation is often the difference between success and failure, between the defeated politician who concedes defeat and disappears and the one who comes back four years later to win the governorship. It's the difference between teams that give up after being swept in the playoffs and those that return a year later to win the championship. It's the difference between two guys who were named by their peers at the Pasadena Playhouse as "least likely to succeed" and years later won Academy Awards—Gene Hackman and Dustin Hoffman.

Motivation makes just as big a difference in the classroom where twenty different children are developing at twenty different speeds with the same material. For that child who is behind, motivation can make the biggest difference of all. When I was a first grader at St. Michael's School in Union, New Jersey, in 1947, there were 94 children in my postwar classroom. Never mind the challenge of teaching the "short A" sound to that many students, imagine the gap between the top and bottom students. So how did Sr. Elizabeth Francis motivate 94 six-year-olds to stay both seated and interested?

As we trooped in from the lunch hour, she would pick up her copy of *Wopsy* and pause until the only sound she heard were heartbeats. And then she'd begin the day's chapter. All these years later, I can still see and hear her standing by her desk, reading aloud. A half century later, I went to the Internet and bought a copy of that short, long out-of-print novel. While the theology of this tale about an apprentice guardian angel struck me as out of date, the richness of the language was remarkable. Most striking of all, though, was the rich contrast between what we were hearing in sister's reading and the simple-minded sentences we ourselves were reading in our Dick and Jane primers.

Hers was the role model, personifying the purpose of all the drill and skill. She offered all of us the hope that if we could master Dick and Jane and the vowels and the meanings, then someday we, too, could work the magic that sister worked with *Wopsy*. As we saw in our teacher, reading really wasn't about worksheets and grades, it was about Wopsy.

So why do we need a book on the subject? Because not all teachers were read to as children and thus need some guidance, because others will need to justify to parents and administrators that they are not wasting valuable "instructional time" with "feel-good time." In this book, Bobbi Fisher and Emily Medvic share more than thirty years' worth of early childhood teaching experience. The accumulation of literary experiences through those decades, complete with their triumphs and failures, is coupled here with the experiences of fellow teachers who also share their read-aloud strategies. How often should one break from the reading in order to ask a question of the class or explain a word in the text? How much discussion before the story, how much after? When is the best time of day for classroom read-aloud?

If indeed reading aloud is the "single most important" literacy event in a child's life, it shouldn't be left to chance or random book choices. If you wouldn't take an expensive vacation trip without an itinerary in hand, taking a class on a journey that will be "carved in stone" needs just as much planning. This volume is your itinerary. Triple A couldn't have done any better.

—JIM TRELEASE

Acknowledgments

We want to thank the "classroom" of people who inspired and helped us to write this book:

All our students to whom we've read aloud; Colin and Abigail, Emily's children, who have heard stacks of stories in their short life times; Jemma and Clement, Bobbi's other grandchildren, who know her as "Gram who reads books"; Jim Fisher, husband and dad, who is always our first editor; Stephen Medvic, husband and son-in-law, who encouraged us every step of the way.

Thanks also to Lois Bridges, our Heinemann editor, who nurtured and supported us through the entire process, and Vicki Kasabian, our production editor, who carefully attended to all the details. Finally, we would like to thank Jim Trelease, who graciously wrote the foreword to this book.

Introduction

This is the second book that we as a mother-daughter team have written together. *Perspectives in Shared Reading: Planning and Practice* (2000) is about teaching literacy using big books and enlarged texts, and it mentions reading aloud as an essential strategy. *For Reading Out Loud: Planning and Practice* specifically addresses reading aloud, which we feel is the most important component in literacy learning. As Don Holdaway so eloquently expressed it, "reading aloud is the foundation of literacy."

Reading aloud has been pivotal to our experiences as parents and as teachers.

> Our experience together with reading aloud began when, as Emily's mother, I read bedtime stories to her and continued throughout the school years, long after Emily had learned to read. During the twenty-five years that I taught kindergarten and first grade, I regularly shared new and inspiring read-alouds with Emily. Now, as a grandmother, I am reading bedtime stories to her two children and to her brother Tim's children. I am known as "Gram, who reads books."
>
> —*Bobbi*

> My recollection of growing up with my mother being a teacher is one of many books and lots of time for reading aloud. She always had a new story to share with my brother and me and we would read aloud throughout the day, at meals, in

the car, and, of course, at bedtime. From as early as I can remember, I lined up my stuffed animals and read to them from a big bag of books from the library. Now, I read aloud to the children in my class at school as well as to my four-year-old son and one-year-old daughter. My mother and I continue to share books and stories as teachers. I call upon her when I need a recommendation for the perfect read-aloud for my classroom. I tell her about a new book that I have read that would be great for a teacher conference.

—*Emily*

This book focuses on reading aloud to prekindergarten, kindergarten, first, and second graders. In it we have included ideas from teachers throughout the country who have shared their favorite read-aloud books and projects, as well as their reasons for making reading aloud an important part of their literacy programs. Aside from relating some of our classroom read-aloud experiences, we have also quoted Jill Ostrow and Kathy Weeks, two of the many teachers who responded to questions about reading aloud in our email survey.

Begin reading aloud a good story and you're on your way to helping children develop as readers and writers and to building a caring learning community.

Imagine a teacher reading *Miss Bindergarten Gets Ready for Kindergarten* (Slate) to her class the first day of school. Everyone laughs together as Miss Bindergarten busily prepares for her first day. The teacher then tells the children what she has done to get their own classroom ready and lets them know that she is always excited and nervous on the first day of school. Next, she invites the children to tell what they did to get ready and how they felt coming to school on their first day.

Then, back to the book: she asks the children to read along with her and they chime right in with "puddle" when she reads, "Tommy Tuttle jumps a ...." During the reading she stops to talk about the different characters in the book who are getting ready for school. "Raise your hand if you rushed to get dressed like Danny Hess." "Put your hand on the top of your head if you hugged someone good-bye like Ophelia Nye." "Yolanda Pound looked around the classroom. What did you notice when you came in this morning?" "Whose name begins with a J like Jessie Sike?"

Throughout this first read-aloud, the teacher and children begin learning about each other and creating a caring community of learners that will continue to grow throughout the year as the children develop as readers and writers. As they meet characters and engage in hearing stories together, they are also gathering experiences that will become part of a shared narrative throughout the year.

The class might revisit Miss Bindergarten if the teacher is out sick. *Miss Bindergarten Stays Home from Kindergarten* (Slate) would be a timely read-aloud with which to start the day when the teacher is out ill. And of course, *Miss Bindergarten Takes a Field Trip with Kindergarten* (Slate) would be a good choice to read the day before a class field trip or even to bring along on the trip. Those teachers who celebrate the 100th day of school may want to hear about the Bindergarten characters again on that special day by reading *Miss Bindergarten Celebrates the 100th Day of Kindergarten* (Slate).

Today many teachers are spending valuable time every day reading aloud to children. They know the many and varied reasons *why* they read aloud (Chapter 1); they know *what* texts to read (Chapter 2); they know *who* might do the reading, *when* to schedule and manage read-aloud times throughout the day, and *where* to create favorable environments in their classrooms where children can listen (Chapter 3); they know *how* to engage children in the process (Chapter 4); they know how to plan appropriate follow-up projects (Chapter 5); and they know how to engage parents in the read-aloud process at home (Chapter 6). Teachers agree with Jim Trelease, who writes, "We read to children for all the same reasons you talk with children: to reassure, to entertain, to inform or explain, to arouse curiosity, to inspire" (Trelease 1995, 8).

1

Why Read Aloud?

We read aloud to children because it is the best way we know to help them learn to love reading. Reading aloud to children forms the foundation of literacy learning. It is an essential component of a balanced reading program in the primary grades, and the groundwork upon which all other elements of a reading/writing workshop are built, including shared reading (using big books), silent reading, one-on-one reading with the teacher, guided reading, paired reading, literature circles, author studies, response journals, and book sharing (see Figure 1–1). Also, reading aloud is an integrative process, one in which children learn about themselves and the world as they learn literacy, gain confidence, and build community (see Figure 1–2).

> I read aloud to my class to share good stories and the excitement of reading (they all love a great story!); to model reading with expression to children just learning to read, so they can see the potential of this new skill they're acquiring; to expose them to book language; to get them to predict what will happen next and then read on so they can confirm their predictions; to do some oral cloze activities; to teach them about different themes we are working on (information input); to show them different ways authors do things, such as using descriptive details, repetitions, and so on.
>
> —*Kathy Weeks*

Elements of a balanced reading program

- reading aloud
- shared reading
- silent reading
- one-on-one reading with the teacher
- guided reading
- paired reading
- literature circles
- author studies
- response journals
- book sharing

Figure 1–1

Reading aloud provides opportunities for literacy learning

Reading aloud supports independence in reading and writing. When we read aloud we model the whys and hows of reading, and children experience what good readers do. Through intonation, expressive emphasis, rhythm and inflection, we invite children to enter the story with us, engaging their imagination and intellect. Through discussions, they connect their own experiences to those of the book characters, relate old ideas to new ones, explore the subtleties of word meanings, and expand their vocabularies. They also develop a sense of story, experience an understanding of characters, themes, settings, and plot and the relationships between them, and learn that successful stories have conflicts and resolutions.

The children hear the patterns of written language in read-aloud literature, and remember them as they become independent readers and writers. When they love a story, they ask to hear it again and again, and in so doing will remember, "Koala Lou, I DO

> **Why read aloud?**
> - Reading aloud provides opportunities for literacy learning.
> - Reading aloud teaches us about ourselves and the world.
> - Reading aloud builds community.
> - Reading aloud promotes gains in confidence.

Figure 1–2

love you!" in *Koala Lou* (Fox); "Purple cat, purple cat, What do you see?" in *Brown Bear, Brown Bear, What Do You See?* (Martin); "and sailed back over a year and in and out of weeks and through a day . . ." in *Where the Wild Things Are* (Sendak); and "I think I can—I think I can—I think I can," in *The Little Engine That Could* (Piper). They will learn to read these favorite books by themselves, and sometimes will include these memorable phrases in their own writing.

> I make sure to leave our read-aloud books out and available for children to reread on their own or with a friend, to refer to for ideas or spelling, or to have nearby in case the class wants to hear it again.
>
> —Emily

Hearing stories and poems read aloud gives children repeated opportunities to hear the sounds of language. As they join in the reading, particularly of books with distinct rhythm and rhyme, they learn to manipulate onsets and rimes. As the children work toward independence in reading, these experiences will support them in making letter-sound correspondences and in creating analogies between familiar and unfamiliar words in print. Children don't need to be able to analyze spoken words into phonemes in order to read. What they do need, and what they get from a rich read-aloud program, is repeated opportunities to hear language, play with it, and join in the reading. In this manner, reading aloud acts as a catalyst for learning to read and write, and moves children more quickly toward reading independence.

Start reading "It's time for bed, little mouse, little mouse, Darkness is falling all over the. . . ." By the time you come to *house,* the last word of the first sentence in *It's Time for Bed* (Fox), the children are filling in the rhyme. After a few readings, they will remember this rhyming phrase and use variations of it as they read and write.

By reading aloud a variety of different books, the teacher is exposing the children to the many ways authors choose to write and tell a story. Through hearing the stories, they learn that books do not all have to begin, "Once upon a time."

> After reading several books over the course of a week, my class decided to examine how each story began. We discussed which openings used "hooks" to draw us in to want to read more and which explained information needed for the plot. Some of our favorite book openings include: "Absolutely everybody in Triple Creek loved their TV sets," in *Aunt Chip and the Great Triple Creek Dam Affair* (Polacco); "With mournful moan and silken tone, itself alone comes one trombone," in *Zin! Zin! Zin! a Violin* (Moss); "It was already Tuesday, and Toot's birthday was on Friday," in *Toot and Puddle: A Present for Toot* (Hobbie); and "One morning, the town mouse woke up shivering from a dream about the kitchen cat who prowled the house," in *Town Mouse Country Mouse* (Brett).
>
> —*Emily*

The more books that are read aloud, the more opportunities the children will have to hear the variety of possibilities they can use in their own writing. They learn that authors have many choices when writing a story or text, such as choices about vocabulary, the beginnings and endings of stories, character descriptions and settings.

Reading aloud teaches about ourselves and the world

Reading aloud generates a love of learning and an interest in the world; it encourages children to want to learn to read. When children are exposed to a rich menu of exciting stories, informational texts, and poetry, they develop a yearning to learn more about their immediate surroundings, as well as environments throughout the globe and beyond. Reading aloud is like taking a field trip. Without leaving the classroom, the children have the common experience of visiting new places, meeting different people, stepping into different time periods, and allowing their imaginations to soar.

An interesting read-aloud is a very effective way to begin a new unit about places you are unable to actually visit.

> In our unit on ancient Egypt, I found I could interest the children by beginning with a few good stories about the country and time period, such as *Tutankhamen's Gift* (Sabuda) and *Pepi and the Secret Names* (Walsh). If possible, I read stories told by or about children the same age as the children in my classroom. The connections to the unit that the children make from hearing stories are stronger than if all they heard or read was from a textbook.
>
> —Emily

> Reading aloud *The Magic School Bus at the Waterworks* (Cole) was the catalyst for the model of the waterworks that my first graders constructed as part of a schoolwide theme on water, and which I describe in *Thinking and Learning Together*. As the project developed, I repeatedly reread the story out loud, and it became impor-

tant as well to have several copies available for independent reading.

—Bobbi

Reading aloud builds community

Read-aloud time gives us the opportunity to become a classroom community. It is a relaxing time when all children can participate successfully at their individual developmental level and in their own unique style. There is no pressure to perform. As we take field trips together through our read-alouds, we make new friends and visit new places. We discuss the feelings of different characters and talk about how they solve problems. This common book experience bonds us together as we share our feelings and help each other solve individual and collective problems.

> One year when I was teaching kindergarten, the day-old chicks that had hatched in our classroom died. Reading *The Tenth Good Thing About Barney* (Viorst) helped the children to express their feelings and talk with each other about what had happened.
>
> —Bobbi

Teachers find it helpful to keep a stack of books on various topics handy in case an event occurs in class that would benefit from a read-aloud. Having the right book at your fingertips is a useful way to address specific subjects that come up in the everyday life of the children we teach, such as the death of a pet, death of a grandparent, losing a tooth, breaking a bone, friendships, moving away, and welcoming a new student. The read-aloud unites the class and is a springboard for the class discussions about the issues affecting the class (see Figure 1–3).

> When one of the children in my class told me she thought another student was making fun of her name, I pulled out *Chrysanthemum* (Henkes) and read it. While the book is a lighthearted look at names and teasing, the talks that followed were quite serious and thoughtful. I believe the discus-

Books for special occasions

- arrival of a new sibling
- breaking a bone or having an injury
- death of a grandparent
- death of a pet
- divorce
- friendship
- losing a tooth
- moving away or moving to a new home
- welcoming a new student

Figure 1-3

> sion was as successful as it was because the book
> was able to bring the class together without
> finger-pointing or making anyone feel defensive.
> While I was reading, the class was able to think
> and listen before starting to talk about the issue.
> —*Emily*

We want the children in our classrooms to love read-aloud time and to consider it a special, comforting experience, regardless of how the rest of the day goes for them. Reading aloud allows children who are struggling to become independent readers, or who have had a difficult time on the playground, or who are excessively active, to be part of the group.

> I remember an extremely active child who often
> had difficulty concentrating in group. And yet,
> when I started to read aloud, he would scoot up
> close to me, eyes and ears focused on the story.
> He did not move a muscle or utter a word during
> the entire reading of *Stellaluna* (Cannon).
> —*Bobbi*

In summary, read-aloud time brings together a class full of individuals and forms a community that shares an enjoyable, enriching, and informative literacy learning experience.

2

What to Read Aloud

When teachers ask, "What should I read?" we respond by telling them to read high-quality literature that they love and that they think the children will love, too. "Engage their hearts and minds," we say. Over time, good read-alouds should address a variety of genre, subjects, and points of view, and introduce children to new subjects, as well as include their current interests and specific book choices. "Read favorite stories over and over again," we tell them. Repeatedly, teachers maintain that their first consideration in selecting a read-aloud is *"Find a great story!"*

Teachers read aloud stories that are humorous and serious, fanciful and realistic, and ones that take place in the past, present, and future. They read alphabet books, poetry, wordless books, books with math problems, and books that talk about music and art. They read fiction, nonfiction, biographies, fables, folktales, and myths. They read stories, as well as newspapers and magazines, that touch on issues important to class members. They read books that describe or include topics of study in social studies and science (see Figure 2–1).

Teachers read different versions of the same favorite story, such as *The Three Little Pigs* and *The True Story of the 3 Little Pigs by A. Wolf* (Scieszka). This practice helps them compare and contrast story elements such as characters, settings, and plots (see Figure 2–2).

> I begin by reading a big book version of the traditional story. Following that, on subsequent days, I read alternate versions and we compare how they are similar and different. We may make a chart showing how each version portrays each

Read aloud different kinds of stories

- humorous
- serious
- fanciful
- realistic
- fables
- folktales
- myths

Figure 2–1

little pig's house, or we may compare the dia-
logue used in each book. After reading *The Three
Little Wolves and the Big, Bad Pig* (Trivizas), our class
discussed what makes a story still fit into the
basic category of a "Three Little Pigs" story.

—*Emily*

Teachers also read several stories by the same favorite
author or illustrator.

When my class particularly enjoyed Patricia
Polacco's *My Rotten Red-Headed Older Brother*, I read
another of her books the next day and then guided the class to look up more of her books. Soon
my class had checked out all of the Patricia
Polacco books from our school library.

—*Emily*

In addition, teachers read stories on a given topic. For
example, as the school year begins, along with *Miss Bindergarten
Gets Ready for Kindergarten* (Slate), they might read *Bernard Goes to
School* (Goodman) or *Minerva Louise at School* (Stoeke). Books about
jazz might include *I See the Rhythm* (Igus), *Duke Ellington* (Pinkney),

**Read aloud different versions
of the same story**

- The Mitten
- The Three Little Pigs
- Little Red Riding Hood
- The Three Bears
- The Gingerbread Man

Figure 2–2

No More! *Stories and Songs of Slave Resistance* (Rappaport), and *The Sound That Jazz Makes* (Weatherford).

Getting started

At the beginning of the year we recommend that teachers read stories that will immediately engage the children so that they get hooked on read-aloud time. These "sure favorites" include stories with familiar settings, such as school and home, stories that are humorous, and stories that the children can enjoy and understand without a great deal of background information or explanation during the reading.

> I kept a stack of favorites in my closet and began with them. I tried to include some that I thought the children might already know, as well as a few that perhaps would be new to them. As the class became accustomed to the procedures and expectations of read-aloud time, I started to vary the subjects and genre and added poetry, informational storybooks, and informational books. I gradually introduced texts that were more complicated or that had unfamiliar contexts and language. I have found that children love to hear

stories, and with our help they can learn to enjoy more sophisticated texts. For example, before I read *The Boy Who Lived with the Seals* (Martin), to my first graders, I gave some background information so they would have a context for this Chinook Indian legend. During the reading, I stopped to check the children's understanding, and to explain and review what was happening.

—Bobbi

Another way to draw children into read-aloud time is to include student choice.

At the beginning of the year I asked the children to bring a favorite storybook from home for us to read in class. This gave me important information about their interests and literacy understandings, and provided a way for them to introduce themselves to their peers. On a chart we listed the book next to the child's name, and then referred to it throughout the year. For example, "Here's a book by Eric Carle, author of the same book that Ryan picked." "This book reminds me of the illustrations in Stephanie's book by Tomie dePaola." If children didn't have books to bring in, I asked them to pick a book that interested them from the school or classroom library.

—Bobbi

Reading different kinds of books

We expand our students' love of learning when we read aloud a variety of texts to them (see Figure 2–3).

Picture books

Most read-alouds in the preschool and primary grades are picture books. Pictures provide visual imagery that help children follow the story, and they link the spoken word to the visual world. Picture books can be read entirely in one sitting. Although the

> ## Read aloud different kinds of books
>
> - alphabet books
> - chapter books
> - counting books
> - picture books
> - poetry
> - rhythmic and rhyming books
> - singing books
> - wordless books

Figure 2–3

majority of picture books that teachers read to young children are fiction or storybooks, they also read informational books, informational storybooks, and poetry. *Strega Nona* (dePaola) is a storybook; *Pyramid* (Macaulay), an informational book; and *The Magic School Bus on the Ocean Floor* (Cole), an informational storybook, in which there is a story line, but also a great deal of scientific information. *Fly Traps! Plants That Bite Back* (Jenkins) has two parallel texts, a story text about a boy who likes plants that eat animals, and an informational text, which tells about carnivorous plants (see Figure 2–4).

Illustrations and photographs are an integral part of most read-alouds in the primary grades. Children hear the text while seeing the pictures that match it. Pictures aid comprehension by helping children make connections between the concrete visual world and the more abstract verbal expression of that world. Sometimes pictures enhance the story by giving details that are not in the text. The illustrations in *The Mitten* (Brett) are filled with details that tell several stories; what's happening to the mitten Nikki dropped; the next animal that is going to get inside the mitten; and what Nikki is doing while this is happening. Once the children notice this about Brett's books, they look up her other books to find the same pattern. When children observe and dis-

General categories for reading aloud

- storybooks
- informational books
- informational storybooks
- biographies
- poetry

Figure 2–4

cuss details in illustrations, they will be more apt to add details to their own drawings to tell their story. Later they will add details in their writing.

Poetry books

There are many poetry picture books—for example, *My Shadow* (Stevenson), *The Midnight Ride of Paul Revere* (Longfellow), or *Casey at the Bat* (Thayer)—that feature a single poem with enriching illustrations, and that we read from cover to cover in one sitting. When we read from an anthology of poems, however, we usually don't read all the poems at once, but enjoy a few at a time, and then return to them at other readings.

> Recently when I read some poems from *Once in the Country: Poems of a Farm* (Johnston) to a first-grade class, the children picked a few to hear from the table of contents.
>
> —*Bobbi*

> I love to find just the right poem for a given moment or lesson. There are great collections of poems about all kinds of topics, including seasons, units of study, and math. When working with fractions, I might begin by reading "Fractions" from *Marvelous Math: A Book of Poems* (Hopkins). This is a collection of short poems that touch on

> many different math concepts. It takes very little time to read before math class and often draws the children in as we begin a new lesson.
>
> —*Emily*

Many poems beg to be read again and again, and often students begin to memorize them. Favorites can be copied or typed for the children to have and read on their own. Of course we want to read a variety of poems throughout the year, not just when we are focusing on poetry as part of language arts time. This way, the children can become familiar with the many different types of poetry. They learn that not all poems rhyme, that some are simply funny and some are rather serious, and that poems can be very short or quite long.

Reading poetry aloud acts as a catalyst for children to write their own poetry, either as their own choice during writing workshop or as part of a poetry writing unit. Certain poetry collections are especially useful to read aloud when introducing children to specific types of poetry that they will be writing. *Leap into Poetry* (Harley) is a collection of twenty-six poems (one for every letter of the alphabet) with a poem providing an example of a poetic form. For example, the poetic form for the letter S is *simile* and the poem is entitled "Silkworm." The poems in A *Poke in the* I: A *Collection of Concrete Poems* (Janeczko) are arranged in visual configurations that match the content of the poem; in this case children need to see the illustrations as they hear the poems.

> I like to read poems from *When Riddles Come Rumbling: Poems to Ponder* (Dotlich) when we have a spare minute or two during the day. This collection contains poems that describe unnamed objects by using clues in rhythmic form. Children think as they listen and try to guess what the poem is about.
>
> —*Emily*

Rhythmic and rhyming books

Babies love to babble and try out different sounds. Toddlers learn nursery rhymes with ease. Primary-age children love hearing books that are rhythmic, and they use such books for support as they work toward reading independence.

> *Chicka-Chicka-Boom-Boom* (Martin) showed me how compelling and engaging the rhythm and rhyme of a meaningful story can be. In the story, the lowercase letters represent children, and the uppercase letters, adults. The children fall and scrape their knees, and the adults pick them up and comfort them. Before I finished the first reading, the children were reading right along with me, filling in with auditory cloze, and participating in the rhythm of the story. This was a favorite book of many of the children in my kindergarten; they could identify with the story and be supported as readers by the rhythmic sound of the language. We read this again and again as a class, and the children often chose it for their independent reading.
>
> —Bobbi

> Children also enjoy a fantasy story by Tedd Arnold, *No More Water in the Tub!* This book is engaging and has a repetitive and rhyming chorus, which gets longer as the story continues. As I read, the story draws the children in and soon they are reading aloud with me.
>
> —Emily

Wordless books

Teachers also "read" wordless books to the class. The children use the pictures in the book to tell the story in their own words. They can also be invited to write the text to accompany their favorite wordless book, individually, with a partner, or as part of a class project.

> Sometimes I directed the children to practice their silent reading as I turned the pages of a

wordless book. "Think the important ideas or story that you see in the pictures." When we started silently reading *Carl Goes Shopping* (Day) the children would become quiet, but as we continued, their faces became animated, and an occasional laugh or giggle would be heard as they "read" the pictures of the dog, Carl, baby-sitting in a department store. Afterwards we told the story to each other in our own words.

—*Bobbi*

Chapter books

Usually beginning in first grade, teachers read chapter books aloud in addition to picture books. Chapter books have few, if any, pictures, so children have to create their own mental images of the story. These books usually cannot be finished at one sitting, so children must be able to remember the story line from reading to reading. Since children can listen to chapter books before they can read them independently, this supportive read-aloud experience, with class retellings and ongoing discussions, gives them strategies for reading chapter books on their own in the future.

Teachers also read aloud chapter books that some of the children can read by themselves. Reading books in series especially encourages this independence. For example, *The Boxcar Children* (Warner), *Henry and Mudge* (Rylant), *The Kids of the Polk Street School* (Giff), the *Magic Tree House* books (Osborne), *Jigsaw Jones Mysteries* (Preller) and *Nate the Great* (Sharmat) often motivate children to seek out the other books to read on their own. Hearing one of the books introduces them to the characters, setting, and general plot pattern (see Figure 2–5).

The first step when deciding on a chapter book is to read the entire book to oneself. Not only must a teacher be sure that the content and vocabulary are appropriate for the class, but he or she should also take the time to be familiar with the characters, tone, and overall feel of the book. This preparation allows the reader to plan for voice changes, make notes of certain places that might call for discussion, and decide where to stop reading each day.

Easy-reader chapter book series

- The Boxcar Children (Warner)
- Henry and Mudge (Rylant)
- The Kids of the Polk Street School (Giff)
- Magic Tree House books (Osborne)
- Jigsaw Jones Mysteries (Preller)
- Nate the Great (Sharmat)
- The Magic School Bus chapter books (Cole)
- Junie B. Jones (Park)
- Little Bill Books for Beginnning Readers (Cosby)
- The Cobble Street Cousins (Rylant)

Figure 2–5

When possible, I try to stop each day's reading at a cliff-hanger or especially interesting spot. (Chapter book authors often put such stopping points at the ends of chapters.) Some days we make predictions about what will happen during the next chapter. Other times, we talk about the section that was just read. I have found it helpful to conduct a very brief review before resuming reading a chapter book each day. We may remind ourselves who the important characters are, or what exciting, mysterious, or troubling event happened at the last reading. If a student was absent the previous day, I might invite a classmate to recap (or summarize) what has taken place in the story. We discuss the concept of main ideas and supporting details. Not only do these short exercises bring all children back into the book, it is also a quick and relevant way to reinforce the story elements. I try to have the review take less than a minute so we can spend most of the time reading.

—Emily

Some books are good read-alouds and some are not. Sometimes I don't know until I've started, and then we decide as a class if we want to continue or not. I like exciting stories with rich characters. Sometimes we read nonfiction as well. It really depends on what we're studying.

—*Jill Ostrow*

Often while I'm reading a chapter book to the class, a student or two will check out the same book from the library. I have had several children want to read ahead to see what is going to happen. They simply can't wait to know how the plot develops and is finally resolved. We do have a class rule: you can't give away the end of the story! Other students simply want to read along with me. They don't read ahead but rather put their bookmark in the book when I do and leave the book in their desk.

—*Emily*

Reading books with different subjects and settings

Multicultural texts

Teachers believe in reading stories that represent the multicultural world we live in. They want to take the children on a variety of field trips that lead them to understand, appreciate, and embrace diversity. Thus, they read stories with characters that represent diverse human beings in a variety of settings. These include characters of different races, ages, sexes, personalities, and occupations, and settings that show the lives, customs, and specific holidays and celebrations of people throughout the world. They read stories that take place during different time periods, and stories set in different locations such as home, school, business, zoo, farm, jungle, city, country, ocean, and outer space (see Figure 2–6).

Read aloud stories with different settings

- taking place in the past, present, or future
- touching on locations familiar to class members (see Figure 1–3)
- providing different cultural settings

Figure 2–6

Math

Choosing the right book can help children see math used in understandable contexts as well as reinforce math concepts. The right read-aloud can help explain math concepts and engage children in thinking mathematically. Introducing a new lesson or reiterating an idea through a read-aloud can be especially motivating.

> I read *Alexander, Who Used to Be Rich Last Sunday* (Viorst) as a jumping-off point to discuss and practice subtracting money. The book tells a funny story while touching on our math concept. Sometimes I simply read the book and then we move on to math manipulatives and our lesson. Other times, the class wants to use our class coins to follow Alexander's money trail, so we reread the book. The children use the manipulatives to "act out" what is happening to Alexander's money while I write the number sentences on the board. Since most of the children are familiar with Alexander from other books, I include *Alexander and the Terrible, Horrible, No Good, Very Bad Day* and *Alexander, Who's Not (Do You Hear Me? I Mean It!) Going to Move* (Viorst) in our read-alouds throughout the day.
>
> —Emily

Read aloud miscellaneous texts

- charts
- letters
- lists
- magazines
- menus
- newspapers
- posters
- programs
- school notices

Figure 2–7

The teacher's own writing

When teachers read out loud stories and poems that they have written themselves, their students experience these important adults in their lives as writers. In sharing how we go about writing, and the difficulties we encounter, and then by asking for suggestions, we model what the process of writing is like for us. When we ask the children for their input, we convey that their suggestions have value and significance. They are not just correcting intentionally incorrect writing but are contributing as writing partners to help us make our piece better. We all become active members of the community of writers in our classrooms.

Nonbook formats

A read-aloud field trip can also include texts that are not books, such as magazines, newspapers, school notices, letters, lists, and performance programs. Many of these readings take less time to finish than a book and are often part of the daily class routine, such as science and social studies charts and posters, notices going home about school and classroom events, and even the lunch menu (see Figure 2–7).

During our weather unit, we read the weather section of our local paper every day. The children got
used to reading charts and pictures that had personal significance to them. They began to notice
trends in weather patterns, and to understand
what the temperature numbers meant to them in
regard to what they ought to wear in order to be
comfortable each day.

—*Emily*

When a historical building we had visited on a
field trip was highlighted in the newspaper a few
months after our visit, I read the article to the
class and we remembered and talked about our
trip. Seeing the photo of the building and hearing
more about it added importance to our visit and
was a great opportunity for review.

—*Emily*

Connecting to state and district standards and curriculum

Teachers across the country are facing new standards with more
testing, and with this comes new emphasis and pressure for
"time on task." As we struggle to ensure we are meeting the
needs of all of our students, as well as addressing town, state,
and national standards, we must not give up our "best prac-
tices." *Reading aloud is a best practice.* Teachers preparing units of
study are particularly looking for unique and interesting ways to
teach the information and concepts required by the mandated
curriculum, and to integrate the content areas with language
arts skills (see Figure 2–8). One of the most effective ways to do
this is through well-chosen read-alouds that can lead to follow-
up readings with discussions, and to meaningful, engaging
hands-on activities.

I have found that I can start a new unit or lesson
best when I begin with a good, related read-
aloud. Not only are children more engaged in the

Read-aloud books about all school subject areas

- art and artists
- math
- music
- social studies
- science
- writing and writers

Figure 2-8

topic, they are also getting another chance to hear a story during the day. I try to find books that are interesting and effective as "jumping-off" tools. A concept does not have to be spelled out to the audience, but merely alluded to or suggested. Sometimes, the subtlety of a concept is more effective than an out-and-out definition because it shows the concept in context and related to other ideas. For example, I introduce the concept of hibernation by initially reading *Blueberries for Sal* (McCloskey) to the class. Although the word *hibernation* is never mentioned in the text, the mother bear in the story tells Little Bear to "eat lots of berries and grow big and fat. We must store up food for the long, cold winter." This classic story is a memorable way to launch a discussion about the types of animals that hibernate, the reasons they do, and how they prepare for hibernation. During this unit on animal life cycles, I also read many texts from several types of genres: informational storybooks (*Tadpoles*, James), fiction (*The Very Busy Spider*, Carle), information (*Big Blue Whale*, Davies) and poetry. I also keep an eye out

for relevant newspaper or magazine articles and
ask my students to do so as well.

—*Emily*

When choosing read-alouds with standards in mind, our
goal is always to find engaging literature on the topic and discuss
the connections while enjoying the story. If we can read a chapter book that relates to the unit, the time is well spent. The children are hearing a good story that reinforces important language
arts skills, while learning more about the topic of study.

In summary, children are in love with the world and can't
wait to find out more about it. Although this chapter has focused
on considerations that teachers might make in choosing what to
read, we emphatically believe that children should also be
involved in the selection. In fact, we acknowledge the incompara-
ble power that a particularly good book has on the individual
child who has made the selection. Regardless of who is choosing,
above all, *find a great story*.

3

Who Reads Aloud?
When and Where?

Who reads aloud?

On a given day in a given classroom, the classroom teacher does most of the reading aloud. It is important, however, for children to experience other adults, as well as other children, reading to them. Different readers bring new and varying voices, reading styles, and interests.

Teachers

When children constantly experience their teacher reading to them, they see how important reading is to that significant grownup in their life. They want to emulate that teacher and become readers themselves. This desire to be a reader is compounded when the children witness others reading, and have opportunities to hear out loud a variety of voice inflections, dialects, expressions, and intonations, and to have conversations about books with people of different cultures, races, occupations, and points of view.

Other adults

Adults feel honored to be invited to read to a class and to share their vocation, hobbies, interests, or favorite childhood story. Although guests often arrive with a favorite book, teachers should be prepared to provide one or two good books for a guest to read. Teachers invite their art, music, gym, and computer teachers, superintendent, principal, custodian, librarian, cafeteria workers, school secretary, nurse, and bus driver to come in

Adult readers: School personnel

- Art teacher
- Bus driver
- Cafeteria worker
- Computer teacher
- Crossing guard
- Custodian
- Librarian or media specialist
- Music teacher
- Nurse
- Physical education teacher
- Principal
- School secretary
- Student teacher
- Superintendent

Figure 3–1

and read their favorite books (see Figure 3–1). They also create schedules for parents to sign up to read, and sometimes ask people from the community such as shopkeepers, town or city officials, firefighters, police, businesspeople, and construction workers (see Figure 3–2).

> I have mystery readers from time to time: my mom, a neighbor, the janitor, the principal, a mom helper, and the kids if they bring a book in to share and want to read it.
>
> —Kathy

Stories on tape

Stories on tape offer a rich resource of read-alouds because they provide easy access to a variety of voices and offer an excellent

Adult readers: Community members

- Businesspeople
- Construction workers
- Firefighters
- Librarian
- Museum employees
- Police
- Shopkeepers
- Town and city officials

Figure 3–2

way for children to experience intonation and expression, which are important aids to comprehension. Aside from using commercial tapes, teachers ask people to tape-record their favorite stories. Bobbi recorded *The Magic School Bus at the Waterworks* (Cole) for Emily during her first year teaching. Emily and her husband recorded *The Royal Dinner* (Parkes) together, using different voices for each character.

Children especially like to recognize their teacher's voice on tape. One teacher we know gives each of the children in her classroom their own tape to record stories they have written or want to read or tell. They love to listen to themselves and each other.

> Occasionally when I make tapes, I give the children a message on the tape before reading the story. I might tell them some interesting things to listen for during the reading. If I am working on the concept of predicting, I stop reading the story before it is over and ask the children to stop the tape and think about, write, or draw what they think might happen at the end. When they are ready, they resume listening.
>
> —*Emily*

Children

Children read aloud throughout the day. During writing time, they read to themselves, their peers and the teacher. As part of writing workshop, they sit in the author's chair and read their work to the class. During reading workshop children read out loud to themselves, in pairs, and in small groups as part of guided reading and literature study. As part of social studies and science they share passages from books as they work on projects and do hands-on experiments. Teachers also make time for children to read to the entire class.

> In my first grade, children signed up on a clipboard if they wanted to read to the class, and usually one child read each day. Sometimes the desire to read was greater than a child's ability to do so smoothly, but allowing the time and creating strategies to support the reader were worth the effort. If children picked books that were too hard, we worked through ways to accommodate: they'd tell the story; I'd read along with them, or read every other page; they'd start the book and I'd finish it; two children would read together, taking turns page by page; they'd have two copies of a book, and one child would read while the other showed the pictures. I found that the children were patient with their classmates and appreciated their efforts. They always clapped at the end of a reading.
>
> —Bobbi

Others in the school love to come in to read.

> When I taught kindergarten I had a schedule sheet outside my door with dates and times for children in the school to sign up to read. Previous kindergartners and children who had siblings in my class were among the most frequent readers. The children in my first-grade class were buddy readers with the fourth graders across the hall.
>
> —Bobbi

The children read aloud to each other all the time. During reading workshop, there can be a lot of out-loud reading. In terms of whole-group read-alouds, when someone wants to share passages from their books, or if they find a book that they want to share with the class, they read it!

—Jill

When to read aloud

In response to the question, "When should I read aloud to my class?" we answer, "Frequently throughout the day," because we believe that frequent read-aloud times have a positive impact on children's literacy learning. When we read frequently we have opportunities for both lengthy, special read-aloud times, and short, informal read-aloud times. Regardless of length, all read-alouds are important learning times.

I usually read aloud after lunch for about twenty-five to thirty minutes. Sometimes I read at the start of the day before we begin our writing if I'm using the book as a jumping-off point for a mini-lesson. Other times I read before we go off for our morning work; I'll use a book to introduce a theme or get the kids excited about what they'll be doing next."

—Kathy

Special read-aloud times

Children look forward to a consistent read-aloud time they can count on every day, and many teachers utilize a specific seg-ment of the school day for this purpose. During special read-aloud times, which last from twenty to forty-five minutes, the class might enjoy a story that will never become an instruction-al class text, or the read-aloud might continue with discussions and introductions to class projects such as readers' theatre, lit-erature study, author study or art, music, or writing projects. Special read-aloud times are held at the beginning of the day, before or after reading or writing workshop, as part of science and social studies, after recess or lunch, and at the end of the day. One teacher told us that she usually reads aloud twice a day. She reads a picture book in the morning after shared reading and before modeled writing, and in the afternoon after recess she reads aloud from a chapter book for about fifteen minutes.

The first story of the day

We believe that what we do to start the school day demonstrates what we value. Since all the other components of a reading and writing classroom build upon the read-aloud experience, we suggest starting each morning reinforcing this foundation by reading a story. This draws everyone together as a classroom community and settles them down on a positive note of learning after the busy morning getting ready for school.

> My own special read-aloud time was at the beginning of the day, setting the tone for the day and signifying that reading aloud was pivotal to learning. No matter what had gone on in the lives of the children that morning before school, we could all gather together for our first "field trip" of the day as we stepped into the learning environment of our particular classroom. Usually I selected a picture storybook that I thought everyone would enjoy, and after reading it, we put it on the library display shelf so the children could read it throughout the day. If available, multiple copies of the book and accompanying story tapes were put in the listening center.
>
> —Bobbi

After recess or lunch

After recess or lunch is a favorite read-aloud time for many teachers. The children come back to the classroom excited and tired after playing and socializing with their peers. Their energy is high, and hearing a story settles them down and reestablishes the classroom community.

I love to have the perfect short book ready to read just as the children are returning from lunch. Children are excited from having social time and need a moment to settle their bodies and minds. Rather than immediately starting a new lesson or directing the children back to work, I read a story that draws them in and refocuses them to the class.

—*Emily*

Before reading and writing workshop, and during social studies or science time

Sometimes the read-aloud will be part of a mini-lesson for reading or writing workshop. For example, *Lilly's Purple Plastic Purse* (Henkes) might be used for character study; *A Cache of Jewels and Other Collective Nouns* (Heller) highlights nouns; *The Snail House* (Ahlberg) is a story within a story; and *Inner Chimes: Poems on Poetry* (Goldstein) is a catalyst for poetry writing. At other times an informational book or informational storybook might be read to introduce or expand upon a social studies or science theme. For example, *Lake of the Big Snake* (Olaleye) is about the African rain forest; *How to Make an Apple Pie and See the World* (Priceman) might be used as part of a geography lesson; *Walk with a Wolf* (Howker) could be read as a text for animal study; *Angel Cat* (Garland) is set throughout the four seasons; and *Rivers: Nature's Wondrous Waterways* (Harrison) discusses the role that rivers play for our planet.

At the end of the day

The end of the day is another favorite reading time. Reading aloud at this time recreates the relaxing atmosphere of the end-of-the-day bedtime story. Many preschool and half-day kindergarten teachers find that this is the best time for them to read to the children, because the rest of the short school day is filled with more active learning experiences.

Since we were usually tired and ready to unwind after a busy day, I found it was difficult to generate discussion at this read-aloud time, but loved the way a story put a positive close to the day.

—*Bobbi*

Some teachers read a chapter from a chapter book at the end of each day. Not only is the time predictable and children can look forward to the next part of the book, but having a set time ensures that the chapter book will be read every day. Planning for continuity is very important when deciding to read a chapter book. Setting time at the end of each day establishes an ongoing reading routine.

> I read from our current chapter book every day at the end of the day. By establishing a set routine, I encourage a calm dismissal. The children know that this is "chapter book time" and they settle in to listen while we wait for afternoon announcements.
>
> —*Emily*

Spontaneous read-aloud times

Along with the dependable daily read-aloud times, unscheduled, spontaneous reading opportunities arise throughout the day. These spontaneous readings save time and minimize behavior problems while providing rich literacy learning. During transition times, instead of waiting for everyone, read to those who are ready. For example, read a poem while the class in lining up to go to lunch, and children are more apt to turn their attention to the text than argue about their place in line (see Figure 3–3).

When a particular situation calls for a spontaneous read-aloud, take the time for it. For example, when someone's tooth falls out, read *Arthur's Tooth* (Brown) or *Trevor's Wiggly-Wobbly Tooth* (Laminack); if it starts to snow, read *Katy and the Big Snow* (Burton), *The Snowy Day* (Keats), or *The Missing Mitten Mystery* (Kellogg).

> One year I announced to the children that I wanted to read to them at least seven different times during the day and that I needed them to help me keep track. Beside our usual reading times, we discovered other suitable read-aloud times for those more spontaneous readings: while waiting to go to lunch we read a small, predictable text; before stopping to clean up I read a short poem;

Spontaneous read-aloud times

- Transition times before
  dismissal
  one subject to another
  lunch
  recess
  specialists
- Settling down times
- Celebrations

Figure 3–3

as we waited to go to art class, we explored a chart; and as children came to the rug ready to go home, we examined a page in an informational text. The leader for the day kept a tally.

—*Bobbi*

I always bring the current chapter book we are reading and one or two picture books on class field trips. I've found it helpful to read aloud to the class while we're waiting for a tour to start, or for the bus driver to return to the bus. Reading aloud is a calming activity. When children are accustomed to listening, they know what behavior is expected. The books are interesting and intriguing to them so they want to listen. I find I don't have to engage in disciplining when I'm reading a good book.

—*Emily*

Where to read aloud

Teachers put a great deal of thought into where they read aloud. Although they usually read in their classroom, many find specific places inside and outside the school building for special read-aloud sessions. Regardless of where we read, we always want the children close to us so everyone can hear the story, see the pictures, and share smiles, laughter, delight, and even sorrow and sadness in the story together.

Teacher choices

Teachers have many decisions to make about the procedures and logistics of reading aloud, many of which depend on the teacher's personality and teaching style, the particular purpose of the read-aloud, the specific classroom context, and schoolwide expectations. Where should the children be? Should they be allowed to lie down or should they sit up? Do they all have to listen? Can they be doing something else while I'm reading? Do I have different expectations for different kinds of reading? When should we go outside to read? How much choice do I want to give the children?

Reading areas

Many teachers have a special reading area in their classroom. One teacher moves a stool around the room and reads in a different space from day to day. If there are pictures she positions herself so everyone can see the book.

> When we read aloud we sit on the couches in our room. The kids don't have desks or specific assigned seats in the room. Instead, we have many comfortable couches and chairs where we meet as a group.
>
> —Jill

> I mostly read aloud at my "meeting area." I also read while walking around the class if the children are working on something at their desks. Sometimes I just sit on the floor with a small group of kids.
>
> —Kathy

> My reading area was lined with shelves and book boxes. Usually the children sat on the car-

peted floor and I sat on a chair. I felt they listened better when they sat up, although sometimes at the end of the day, when everyone seemed tired, they were allowed to lie down. Occasionally the children drew while I read. Then they sat at their tables or used clipboards at the reading area.

—*Bobbi*

Organizing a read-aloud library

Teachers know that when the reading materials in their classroom are well organized, their daily routine and curriculum plans are more effective. They want reading materials accessible so when a particular topic comes up, they can quickly find the appropriate book to read aloud. They also want their students to be able to find a familiar book, locate books on a topic of interest, or easily discover a new book.

One way to facilitate easy access is to store books on a particular subject in the corresponding center in the room; that is, math books in the math center, science books in the science area. Although the standard learning areas in a primary classroom are math, reading, science, social studies, and writing, literacy can be enhanced by displaying books in other areas, such as at the workbench, sand table, puppet theatre, and block or construction area. Dramatic play areas are also enriched when books become part of the environment, as described in *Joyful Learning in Kindergarten* (Fisher 1998).

I stored books in cardboard or plastic boxes and labeled each box with a particular topic. For example, in the science area there were boxes for books about reptiles, mammals, planets, trees, experiments, and so on. Social studies categories included maps and geography, the continents, and specific curriculum areas such as westward expansion. In the writing area we stored dictionaries and fiction and nonfiction books about journal writing.

—*Bobbi*

> I keep plastic tubs of books in the middle of the
> desks. At the beginning of the year I put a variety
> of books in each tub and the children select from
> the tub at their table at silent reading time. They
> add their own choices, and throughout the year
> we include unit-related books, chapter books, or
> class-made books.
>
> —*Emily*

Reading aloud to young children above all involves reading
picture storybooks. Organizing them can be a challenge as classroom libraries grow. Some teachers sort the books alphabetical-
ly into boxes or label a shelf with the letters of the alphabet so
books can be stored according to the author's last name. Others
organize according to the first letter of the title, with the inten-
tion that their students will begin to learn to return the book to
the proper place.

Another recommended way is to organize picture books
according to the popular read-aloud topics in the classroom.
Categories might include alphabet, wordless, singing, poetry,
and books about friendships, birthdays, animals, or specific
countries or cultures throughout the globe. Teachers create their
own categories, but children will become more engaged in reading when they are involved in creating some of the groupings,
labeling the boxes, and adding the books (Fisher 1995).

Displaying the cover of a new or familiar book entices children to pick it up and explore it. On a regular basis we rotate the
books that are displayed in each area of the room. Sometimes we
place a puzzle, stuffed animal, or puppet that corresponds to the
book's character with the book.

Our purpose is keeping books well organized so we can find
a particular book we want to read, engage children in books, and
create a sense of order for learning. Although we want orderly
bookshelves, we have to remember that the children are more
interested in finding or hearing a good book. We believe it is
important to involve the children in the process, but as teachers
have told us, every day after school they spend some time keeping the organization in order.

In my closet I keep a pile of favorite books that I know I'll want to bring out for special read-aloud times during the year. Then after I read a book, I add it to the class library.

—*Emily*

In considering who, when, and where to read aloud, teachers strive to create a combination of consistency and variety. The classroom teacher does most of the reading at established times in a fixed area of the room. Within this routine, however, they ask others to read, they read throughout the day, and they continually devise unique places for children to hear a good story.

4

How to Read Aloud

There are many considerations that go into how teachers read aloud. The first reading of a story sometimes differs from subsequent readings. The discussions before, during, and after reading are planned carefully by teachers, but readings also provide spontaneous conversations generated by the children. There are different strategies for reading picture books and chapter books. Also, we read fiction differently from nonfiction, and serious texts differently from humorous ones.

Finding a reading style

When we hear an adult read a children's book out loud, we notice the uniqueness of the reader's style. For example, some readers regularly change expression and intonation; others employ a steady tone. Some take on the role of the characters; others maintain a narrative voice. Some move back and forth and involve their bodies; others remain still. Different reading styles reflect the different personalities of readers, and all can be effective.

Whenever possible, read a chosen story out loud to yourself before reading it to the class. It is especially important that you read a chapter book ahead of time so you can tell if it fits the needs and interests of the class, and so that you won't be surprised by some of the language or events in the text.

As you read, ask yourself the following questions: Am I reading too fast or too slow? Do I look at the audience enough? Does my expression enhance the text? Do I interrupt too often for discussion? When should I clarify difficult points or vocabulary during the reading? What will the children be doing while I'm reading? When will they pay closest attention?

The first reading

Usually the first time we read a book or poem to the class we try to read it through with few interruptions because we want everyone to hear the entire text as the author wrote it. Consider Mem Fox and her story *Tough Boris*. She carefully chose the words and crafted them together, and we need to hear her creation. Any explanation of ours would interrupt the sound and flow of her storylike poem. As the children listen to *Tough Boris*, their minds weave her words with their own experiences to make their own meaning, and as teachers we do not want to interrupt their thought process. Although we might discuss the context of the story beforehand and return to the text later for further discussion, during the first magical reading, our experience is mostly with Mem Fox and Tough Boris.

> We didn't discuss every book that I read to the class. I always remembered how my own children listened raptly to those stories that I read to them at bedtime. When I finished, no one needed to say anything, and yet I knew the experience had been meaningful. I continually remind myself that just because I didn't "teach" something, it didn't mean that the children were not learning.
>
> —Bobbi

Exploring a picture storybook

Sometimes teachers discuss a read-aloud text in detail, discussing it before, during, and after the reading.

Before reading

There are many ways to explore a book before reading it aloud. Some of the questions to ask yourself before introducing a storybook are

1.   What background knowledge do the children have or need for a successful reading?

2. From the title and cover illustrations, can we predict what the story is about?

3. Should we take time to tell our personal stories and how the story relates to our lives?

4. On what curriculum areas do I want to focus?

5. What skills or strategies do I want to emphasize?

6. What reading/writing connections do I want to make? Should we discuss the title, author, illustrator, publisher, copyright, dedication page? Why do we think the author wanted to write this book? What did he or she need to know in order to write it? (This discussion can also follow the read-aloud.)

7. If this is a first reading, do I want to read it through without discussion, or do I want to begin an in-depth conversation?

8. Do I want to ask the children to examine the book for a particular purpose?

One teacher gave us a list of some of the ways that she introduces a book. She and the class look at the cover and title page, talk about the author, predict what they think the book might be about, talk about other stories by the same author or that have the same theme, and discuss how the book relates to what they are studying or how it connects to their lives. Then they go through the book and look at the pictures, read the chapters titles aloud, and think about what each chapter might be about.

During reading

We always want to be careful that during the first reading of a book, any discussion will not detract from the understanding and appreciation of the story. Sometimes, however, we explain vocabulary as we read along, or model and think aloud about the story. Occasionally it is beneficial to have short discussions to make sure the children understand what is happening. One teacher told us that as she begins to read, she ask her students to create a "picture in their heads," and then compare it with the pictures in the book.

> During preparation for a read-aloud, sometimes I
> use Post-its and write myself reminder notes; I
> stick them where I want to discuss or draw atten-
> tion to a part of the book.
>
> —*Emily*

Some questions to ask yourself as you plan the read-aloud are

1. Where in the story might I need to clarify what is happening? Is there vocabulary that we need to understand as we
   read along? Do I want to ask questions to check the children's comprehension of the story?
2. Are there places in the story where I might pause in the
   reading so the children can predict what will happen next?
3. Are there places where I want to stop and discuss new concepts and extend the children's understanding?
4. Where and when should I encourage children to talk and
   express their ideas?
5. If we decide to read this book again and use it as a core text
   for study, what might be some further discussion points?

After reading

> After I read the final page and close the book, I
> usually pause and keep silent. I want us to be
> with our own thoughts before we talk and some-
> times there is no further conversation.
>
> —*Bobbi*

Follow-up discussion depends to a large extent on what has
happened during the reading. Some of the questions teachers
might ask themselves are

1. Should we have an immediate follow-up discussion?
2. Should we review our predictions now that we have heard
   the story?
3. How should the discussion begin? During the reading I lead
   most of the discussion, but the children are more in charge

of the follow-up. My best initial question is, "What did you notice?" This open-ended question gives everyone a chance to answer and realize that their response is valid and valued. It gives me the opportunity to hear the connections they have made and to plan next steps. I also might ask them what they learned, what surprised them in the book, what they did and didn't like in the story, what the book got them thinking about, and what other books they were reminded of.

4. How should the discussion continue? The children's initial responses help me to develop a more in-depth discussion. Should we read the story again? Should we do a follow-up project?

5. Do we want to read other versions of the same story, or other books by the same author?

6. What are the possibilities for follow-up activities?

> I ask the kids if they liked the story and why or why not. Sometimes I call on children to answer and other times they tell a classmate. We may discuss what we would have done differently or the same if we were the author, or compare what happened in the story to our own circumstances. Sometimes we do a follow-up book in response.
>
> —Kathy

Discussing a chapter book

Many of the same strategies for reading a picture book can be applied to chapter books as well. Although it is not possible to complete a chapter book in one day, it is important to take care not to lose involvement in the story by stretching out the reading over too many days. Since we want everyone in the class to stay involved, we suggest you try to read at least one chapter a day.

Questions to consider when reading aloud a chapter book:

1. Have I read the entire book to myself to be sure it is appropriate for my class?

2. Do I want to create follow-up opportunities at the end of the book?

3. Will I be able to devote enough consistent time to read the whole book in an amount of time that will enable the children to follow the story line?

4. Have I checked the calendar to avoid having a vacation in the middle of reading the book?

5. Do I want to give the children a choice of several chapter books or do I want to choose the book?

6. Have I noted a few discussion-starting questions for various points in the book?

7. Are there parts in the book that may require some explanation?

8. Have I noted where I can stop reading each day that will be particularly exciting or an enticing "cliff-hanger"?

> Before we begin I always ask, "Where were we in the book?" and we talk about what was going on. During the reading, I'm reading and the kids are listening. Sometimes we might need to stop and talk about something that was read, but usually we just read. At the end we talk about the story.
> —Jill

Exploring nonfiction

Although in the preschool and primary grades teachers read aloud a preponderance of fiction, they also include a variety of nonfiction. Young children are intensely inquisitive about the world, and they have the ability to learn and integrate a great deal of information. Most storybooks have a beginning, middle, and end, and can be read straight through with minimal comments and explanation. Informational (nonfiction) books, on the other hand, have many different formats, and invite us to read selected sections with frequent stops for discussion during the reading. Most nonfiction texts for young children are written in the form of informational storybooks, which include a combination of story line and information and are usually read from beginning to end, but with discussion throughout.

Nonfiction texts should be available to the children for reference purposes. Many children's nonfiction books have pictures with diagrams and charts. These graphics require a closer look by individuals or a small group after a read aloud.

> I have found that nonfiction texts are great to use when there are just a few moments for a read-aloud. For example, I have a pile of books to pull from while we are waiting to be called to an assembly or to the buses. When there isn't enough time to launch into something new or even to finish a trade book, I read a page from a nonfiction text like *Disguises and Surprises* (Llewellyn). This book contains very interesting, unusual (and captivating) facts about how some animals and insects camouflage themselves. Each animal has two or three pages, with pictures devoted to its unique life. Sometimes we have time to read about just one animal, other times we can read several sections. Reading this type of book engages the children during those "waiting" moments.
>
> —*Emily*

Questions to ask yourself in planning and reading an informational text or informational storybook are

1. Do I want to read this through from beginning to end? If so, how much can we read and discuss in one sitting?
2. Do we want to read this for certain information? If so, will we use the table of contents and/or index?
3. Do we want to read several different texts and make cross-references?
4. How does this book relate to what we are studying in science or social studies?
5. What follow-up projects might be generated from this book?

Every teacher can read aloud successfully. Preparing to read aloud by reading the chosen texts ahead of time, planning for discussion, and reflecting on your own reading style will make the read-aloud times even more worthwhile and enjoyable.

5

Follow-up Projects

Literature-rich classrooms provide a variety of opportunities for children to build upon the foundation of read-aloud experiences and to explore new ideas and interests through follow-up projects. As children learn more about themselves and the world, they make new connections and integrate current learning with established knowledge. They develop this integration through discussions and projects in the form of retellings (telling the same story), innovations (using the same story structure but a different context), and extensions (continuing the story where it left off).

Follow-up projects, which are often integrated with social studies and science curriculum, take many forms, including writing, art projects, music, movement, drama and puppet shows, mathematics, and dramatic play environments (see Figure 5–1).

> We may create a Venn diagram together, comparing the book I've just read to another. I might have children illustrate their favorite part or characters or draw/write about the event they think was the scariest, saddest, most exciting, and so on. If it's a chapter book, I may have them draw/write about a possible ending before we get to it. We also may act out a book we've read together or do a story innovation together as a class (I write, they provide the ideas). These innovations once inspired a student to take *The Three Little Pigs* and turn it into *The Three Little Penguins and the Big, Bad Leopard*

Follow-up projects

- art projects
- community outreach
- dance
- dramatic play environments
- movement
- mathematics
- music
- puppet shows
- readers' theatre
- science experiments
- TV or radio show
- writing

Figure 5–1

Seal—a student's idea, not mine! We also have made "wall stories" that tell about our read-aloud in pictures or writing.

—Kathy

Reading aloud was an integral component of the dramatic play environments that the children and I created in kindergarten. As we began to set up an environment, I would read fiction and nonfiction and the children would incorporate the information and concepts into their play in the environment. For example, as I describe in *Joyful Learning in Kindergarten*, the books I read aloud about fish and aquariums added to the decor of our aquarium and the children's role playing as fish.

—Bobbi

Class books

Many of the follow-up projects in primary classrooms involve creating class books, either as a retelling, innovation, or extension. Students develop a library of class books as reminders of texts that they have enjoyed throughout the year. These books are authentic reading materials and effective writing models for everyone. They can be read at school and taken home to share with family and friends.

In one classroom, children made up their own innovation of *If* . . . (Perry). The phrases, "If toes were teeth . . . If fish were leaves . . . ," along with the illustrations, generated a great deal of discussion and ignited the children's imagination to make up their own sayings and pictures. After reading each chapter of *The Boxcar Children* (Warner), in a second-grade class, one group retold the story, another illustrated it, and together they bound the chapter pages into a book. As part of an author study on Bill Peet, one teacher did a model writing of her own Bill Peet story in front of the class, and then the children wrote their own.

> One year we made a class book of the important stories that we read aloud. Each page listed the title, author, illustrator, publisher, copyright, a memorable phrase from the book, and an accompanying picture. For example, the child assigned to the storybook of the poem *Life Doesn't Frighten Me* (Angelou) drew a scary picture of someone alone in bed at night to accompany the sentence, "That doesn't frighten me at all."
>
> —Bobbi

> After reading the big book I *Spy* (Drew) together, our class decided to create our own I *Spy* book. The children thought of an animal to describe using the same format from the book. On the front of a folded piece of paper, they wrote about their creatures without naming them but gave enough clues so a reader could guess what they were writing about. The children drew their ani-

mals and labeled them on the inside of the paper and then cut holes for the eyes. We bound all of the pages together for a class version of I S*py*.

—Emily

Author studies

Studying the books and illustrations of favorite authors is another successful way to engage children in the love of reading and writing.

In my classroom we became involved in an in-depth discussion of the characteristics of Jan Brett's work, and her unique way of using language. The children compared her work to those of other authors and to themselves as writers. For example, "I'm just like Jan Brett—I like elves, trolls, and woodland animals" (*Trouble with Trolls*). Conversations such as this became habit forming, as we generated interest and information about other books and authors: "My mom just had a baby. I'm going to write a story about my new baby sister just like Tomie dePaola did in *The Baby Sister*."

—Bobbi

One year my class looked closely at Kevin Henkes' books. The children liked the handwritten quotes in the illustrations and began adding that feature to their own work. After noticing that a few of the characters were in several books, we decided to read his collection of books in the order that they were published. This was also a great natural lesson in dates and locating the copyright information.

—Emily

Many authors have websites that students can visit to acquire more information about the author's background, learn about other books by the same author, play games, and take an in-depth look at the content and context related to some stories. (We suggest that teachers visit the sites themselves before recommending them to students.)

Readers' theatre

Readers' theatre includes different ways that children read poems and stories to a larger audience. Presentations can be brief, such as reading and performing a favorite poem as suggested in *Wham! It's a Poetry Jam* (Holbrook), or can be more complicated, as described in the following readers' theatre of *Make Way for Ducklings* (McCloskey).

Each year a second-grade teacher we know has her class perform a readers' theater of *Make Way for Ducklings*. Children are individually responsible for memorizing several lines of the story and knowing where their parts come in. When they perform in front of the school, they sit on the steps of the stage and stand up and recite when they come to their parts. The children learn literacy skills and strategies as they get to know the story through purposeful repetition. This cooperative endeavor draws them together as a learning community, and fosters individual and class pride. Children who performed the story when they were in second grade love to hear it as third, fourth, and fifth graders.

> One year we created a readers' theater to perform on one of our Visitor Days (described in my book *Thinking and Learning Together*). I enlarged the text of *Arrow to the Sun* (McDermott), glued it to a piece of cardboard from a big box, and had each student pick a favorite line to read as part of our museum performance.
>
> —Bobbi

Hands-on projects

Many books offer opportunities for hands-on extensions, but by no means does this mean that a project should be done with every book read aloud. Teachers need to decide when and whether to create a follow-up activity. They want to be certain that the project has literary and educational value and doesn't detract from the children's enjoyment of the story itself.

> After reading *Mouse Paint* (Walsh), my first graders experimented with mixing primary colors. They used food coloring and petri dishes and recorded their results on an experiment form that I made. One teacher has her children paint like mice to tie in an art project to the book.
>
> —Bobbi

> My class made colored ice cubes (using food coloring) of primary colors after reading *Mouse Paint*. The students put two different-colored ice cubes in a Ziploc bag and predicted and then recorded what color the water would be when the ice melted.
>
> —Emily

In another classroom, after the reading of *Wilfred Gordon McDonald Partridge* (Fox), the children wanted to make memory boxes. They decorated shoeboxes and filled them with memories of kindergarten to take home at the end of the year.

Math

Math read-alouds provide an excellent way to introduce new math topics, offer another explanation for a concept, or suggest a jumping-off point for a hands-on math lesson. There are many books that are written well and created as "math concept" books. For example, children enjoy the MathStart books by Stuart J. Murphy. (This series is divided into three levels, from preschool to grade 3.) Each book is devoted to one math concept that is explored through a story and followed by suggestions for further exploration.

> My class loved *Betcha!*, a story about two boys who count things around them. One estimates while the other tries to count each object. There is a sur-

> prise ending, which makes the story a good read-aloud while introducing the concept of estimation versus one-to-one counting. After reading it I have a variety of estimation tasks for the children to do. Using a read-aloud makes the introduction of this lesson smooth, interesting, and meaningful.
>
> —*Emily*

> I've read *Math Curse* (Sczieska) to encourage my children to write their own math word problems and *Measuring Penny* (Leedy) to examine the variety of ways there are to measure things. *Counting on Frank* (Clement) is a funny book that explores all kinds of math problems that can be found in everyday life.
>
> —*Emily*

Again, the important thing about using a trade book during math is first to find an interesting story or text. Reading a contrived story that mentions math is not going to be effective, nor is it going to hold the children's attention.

Addressing standards and testing

Many of today's curriculum and testing standards require that students be familiar with and comfortable using and identifying the various elements of a story, such as setting, character, sequence of events, plot, and problem and resolution. Although standardized testing formats often require the children to identify these elements in isolation, they can be taught through reading good literature. In our book *Perspectives on Shared Reading* (Fisher and Medvic 2000), we describe ways to include testing standards and curriculum guidelines through using big books. Many of these strategies are applicable for the reading aloud of trade books as well.

Change the element

In order to help students understand the importance and impact each element has on the overall story, we use a short read-aloud and invite students to choose one element to change.

> After reading *Watch Out! Big Bro's Coming!* (Albo-
> rough), I ask the students to rewrite the story as if
> it took place in a different habitat. (Habitats is
> one of my state-required topics of study.) For
> example, instead of the jungle, what if the setting
> was around a pond? What parts of the story could
> remain the same? Which parts would be differ-
> ent? Would the ending change? Which animals, if
> any, could still be in the story? What animals
> could be added in place of the current characters?
> —Emily

This same activity can also be performed by changing a
character from young to old, from mean to nice, or by changing
the time frame from the past, present, or future. It does not lend
itself to every book, and it seems to work best with short stories.

What if?

A variation on "change the element" is for students to choose a
major event in the story and describe what might have happened
if that event had occurred earlier in the story, later in the story, or
had not even happened at all. For example, what if the man with
the beret had not noticed Corduroy in his laundry bag and had
taken him home by mistake (*A Pocket for Corduroy*, Freeman)? What
if, in Jan Brett's *The Mitten*, the bear had come upon the mitten
first, before all of the other animals? Thus, while discovering
about sequence of events, cause and effect, and other literary
elements that are addressed in curriculum standards and standardized testing, the children are also enjoying the speculation
and using their imaginations.

Returning to books

We suggest that after reading a book to the class, teachers make
it available to the children to look at again on their own, with
opportunities to reread the book by themselves or in pairs. Less
fluent readers enjoy retelling the story based on the pictures and
what they remember from listening to the reading. Regardless of
their independent reading proficiency, most students love to go

back to the book to study the pictures more closely. For example, Jan Brett's illustrations beg to be examined again and again because Brett creates a second, parallel story in the margins of her books.

> One of my students noticed the picture story that was unfolding in *Gingerbread Baby* (Brett) and decided to write down what Mattie was doing while the gingerbread baby ran away.
>
> —*Emily*

Encouraging children to take another look at a read-aloud book also gives them the opportunity to clarify questions they had during the reading as well as delve deeper into the text.

> After reading *Abe Lincoln* (d'Aulaire) to my second graders, one of my students came up immediately and wanted to be the first to get to look at the book. This particular biography, which we read over two days, is a long text with detailed pictures. Marshall started at the beginning and read the book paying close attention to the pictures in the side margins. He stopped at the pages that described how Lincoln was killed and looked at the illustrations to help him picture the scene. This book became Marshall's favorite book for a while. He referred to it again and again and asked if he could keep it on his desk. Although the written text was more difficult than his independent reading level, he enjoyed reading it. It may not have been a book he would have picked up on his own because its length might have seemed too overwhelming for him. I believe that the read-aloud was the key to getting him to pursue the text further.
>
> —*Emily*

In our experience, independent reading is one of the most advantageous times during the school day for children to return to those books that have been read aloud. As Bobbi describes in *Thinking and Learning Together*, a daily routine of independent "silent" reading provides children opportunities to explore favorite books, as well as gives the teacher uninterrupted time to read one-on-one with students.

> One year the children started arguing over certain books that everyone seemed to want to read during "silent reading" time. It seemed that some children were hiding specific books (*Go Dog Go!*, Eastman; *The Signmaker's Assistant*, Arnold) so that they could find them before independent reading. Consequently, we developed a list of the "popular books," and decided to give them to the leader for the day.
>
> —Bobbi

> I have a special shelf where we keep recently read read-alouds so that those books will easily get back into the hands of children for more in-depth scrutiny.
>
> —Emily

In summary, although teachers initiate many follow-up projects, we believe that children should be given a great deal of choice within them, and whenever possible, be allowed to generate their own. Additionally, it is always important to keep in mind that follow-up projects should not take the place of read-aloud time or independent or peer reading.

6

Parents and Reading Aloud

Why encourage reading aloud at home?

Teachers know how important reading aloud is for children. The more stories that children are exposed to at home, the more opportunities they will have for hearing rich language, learning new vocabulary, grasping story structures, and developing a love of reading. In his work on early literacy, Don Holdaway (1979) discovered that children who were read to at home came to school with a strong literacy set necessary for gaining independence in reading. The *Reading Together Parents' Handbook*, included in each set of the *Reading Together* series for ages three, four, and five, claims, "Reading aloud is one of the most important ways you can help your child learn to read and write—and it's never too early to start" (Barr and Ellis 1998).

Reading aloud every night (and throughout the day) fosters a good reading routine.

> In our house, it is just a given that the last thing our children do before going to bed is hear several stories. My son sometimes wants to be surprised by what books are read. Other nights he creates a stack of favorites. Following a trip to the library, we read our new library books. If he is particularly interested in something, we'll find as many books on the topic as we can and read those. (One night, we read ten books that all had

to do with baseball!) Sometimes we will read a couple of chapters from our current chapter book. Regardless of the books, the routine is the same: we read together.

—*Emily*

Reading aloud at home shows children how important reading is in everyday life, and that it is not just something done at school. Children will begin to notice that all family members read a variety of texts for a variety of reasons: the newspaper, magazines, letters, recipes, directions, bills, and school notices, to name a few, as well as books.

Reading aloud at home creates time for parents and child to spend together in a warm, positive, and calm way.

The parent of a kindergarten child shared with me that although she and her son had many disagreements and conflicts throughout the day, the bedtime story always brought them together and enabled them to release much of the tension.

—*Bobbi*

Reading aloud confirms the constancy of print. As children are read the same books over and over, they begin to recognize that the exact same story with the same words is read every time, no matter who the reader is. Often a favorite read-aloud becomes the first book that a child reads independently. The memorized text supports the young reader as he or she begins to attend to the text and read word for word.

The more stories or texts a child hears, the wider his or her repertoire of knowledge and ideas. Children learn vocabulary, story structure, and grammar and expand their knowledge about the world through listening to books or other texts (see Figure 6–1).

Creating a positive atmosphere

It is important for parents to keep the read-aloud time positive so that children are not turned off. Following are some suggestions for keeping the time joyful.

Benefits of reading aloud at home

- helps to develop a love of reading as the child learns to read
- fosters a good reading routine
- shows the importance of reading in everyday life
- creates a warm, positive, and calm experience between parent and child
- confirms the constancy of print
- helps to expand the child's knowledge and understanding of the world

Figure 6-1

Reading aloud at home should not be "quiz time"

While it is important to discuss a book with a child, we encourage parents to take care not to ask "quiz" questions. First, if a child thinks that the parent is going to ask a series of questions following a read-aloud, he or she may listen just to remember facts in anticipation of being quizzed. Second, students are asked plenty of questions at school! Read-aloud time at home should primarily focus on *enjoying a good story or text together*! Too much quizzing will result in children who don't want to listen to read-alouds.

The adult remains the prominent reader

Parents should be encouraged to continue reading aloud to their children even after they have learned to read. We know that since children's independent reading lags behind their ability to comprehend complicated stories and concepts, adult reading, accompanied by discussion, will enrich the learning potential. Also, children have been thinking and working all day in school. What more relaxing way to end the day than to hear a good story or listen to the next chapter of an absorbing book? We have found that a good rule of thumb is to let the child choose who will read.

Creating a positive environment

- Reading aloud at home should not be "quiz time"
- The adult remains the prominent reader
- Keep the child's reading stress-free

Figure 6–2

Keep the child's reading stress-free

For those times when the child has taken over the role of reader, we remind parents how essential it is to create a stress-free environment, one that does not discourage the child from wanting to read or that results in a dislike of reading altogether. Parents should be aware of how they listen to their child. Are they getting irritated at miscues, or are they being helpful? Are they focusing more on individual words that the child is reading, rather than listening to the meaning of the story? Are their body language and verbal comments positive? (See Figure 6–2.)

Building a home or classroom library

Building a library of children's books is important. Parents and teachers ask, Where should I start? How much will I have to spend? Do books always have to be new? We offer the following suggestions to both parents and teachers as they start or add to a home or classroom library.

Trips to the library

Most public libraries are very generous about the number of books a family can check out at one time, and many allow teachers to take out one book per child in their class. Usually books for a classroom can be checked out for an entire month.

> At the public library each month I filled a canvas bag with twenty-five (easy number to remember) books on a variety of topics that addressed the

interests of my students and that related to our current areas of study. After Emily read them at home, I took them to school and spent a half-hour or so showing the books to the class. We'd all sit on the rug and one by one I'd take a book from the bag and we'd read the title, look at the cover, and leaf through it. Then I'd hand it to someone who wanted to read it for the silent reading that was to follow.

—*Bobbi*

Book clubs

Book clubs sponsored through school are a tremendous asset to teachers and parents. The monthly catalogs of these clubs are full of inexpensive educational books and materials to order (audio- and videotapes, puppets, stickers, and more).

I send forms from several book clubs home every month with ordering instructions. I have found that if the ordering date is consistent every month, parents will know when to turn in their orders and when they will receive the books. Although it can be awkward to ask parents to spend money, I encourage every parent to order something at least once during the year. In the few cases when parents have not been able to order books, I have used my bonus points to order them for the children.

—*Emily*

I wrote the date that the form was due on the top of each order form so that children would not be disappointed by bringing it in after I had placed the order.

—*Bobbi*

We stress to parents that one of the best ways to encourage reading is to find books on topics that interest their children, and that participating in a school book club is one of the easiest ways to do this. In order to give children ownership in the selection of books, we suggest that parents let their child go through the catalogs and circle the books he or she would like and then talk together about the choices. (Parents can set a dollar limit that the child should not exceed.) This sense of ownership is evident when the newly ordered books are delivered to school. Some children hold their prizes as if they were precious pieces of art, some write their names neatly inside the cover, and most can't wait to read and share them with their friends.

Library and yard sales

Library and yard sales are easy places to pick up inexpensive used books. (Be sure to flip through the books to make sure there aren't any missing or badly damaged pages.) Children don't mind hearing a story from a used book. (In fact, there is something pleasurable about rescuing an old book and enjoying it.) Contact your library and find out if they hold book sales. Usually children's books range from ten to fifty cents apiece. Arrive early, for the good ones are the first to go!

Bookstores

Just visiting the children's area of a bookstore is inspiring and exciting. You can imagine the possibilities for your classroom, both in terms of books and physical setup.

> I make a point of spending time perusing the new books and scanning the shelves for titles to add to my collection, for both school and home. Before I purchase any new book, I usually jot down the title and author and try to check it out of the library. That way I can test them out with my own children and with my students at school. If I find one that is a must-have, a great read-aloud, then I will make the investment.
>
> —Emily

Donations for the classroom

One way to expand your classroom library is to provide families with opportunities to donate a special book. Instead of holiday gifts to the teacher, students might pick a favorite book and donate it to the class. On their birthday, children might like to present a book to the class, and write their names inside it as a reminder of who gave the gift.

Volunteer readers

Parents want to be involved in their child's world at school. Specifically, they would like to spend time in their child's classroom, and we have found that young children feel proud and nurtured when their parents join the classroom for a morning. Asking parents to read aloud to individuals, small groups, or the entire class is an excellent way to include them in the classroom.

> My goal is to include as many parents as possible to help in the class during the year. I have a parent section in my monthly class newsletter where I give a "call for volunteers." Reading aloud is one of the choices I offer parents. For those unavailable during school hours, many agree to make a book on tape.
>
> —*Emily*

Reading with individual children or small groups

> I encouraged parents to spend a morning in class with their child. Some planned an art project for a small group, but many were happy to read. With clipboard in hand, the child of the visiting parent took charge of getting classmates to sign up and of keeping the schedule going throughout the morning. Individual readers decided if they wanted to read to the parent or if they wanted to hear a story, and if they wanted to read alone or with a group of friends. Sometimes parents brought in a favorite book, but if the child was the reader, he or she chose the book.
>
> —*Bobbi*

Reading aloud to the class

> I find it best to provide a list of books from which guest readers can choose, so that I know the reading is both age and content appropriate for my class. Usually, parents welcome the suggestions and defer to the teacher as the professional. I encourage parents to take a book home ahead of time to practice reading it with their child before reading it to the class.
>
> —Emily

> I encouraged parents to collaborate with their child when selecting a book to read to the class. Experience taught me the benefits of checking over the book before the parent began reading.
>
> —Bobbi

Making books on tape

Some parents are delighted to make a book on tape for the class. Usually the parent provides the tape and the teacher offers several titles from which the parent can choose. The teacher then sends the book home along with a list of tips for making books on tape. For example:

- Read the book aloud to yourself and your child a few times before taping. It is very important that you are familiar with what you are reading.
- Be sure to read the title and the names of the author and illustrator.
- Read slowly. The listener needs to hear all of the words, but the reading should be fluent, not stilted.
- Pause at the end of each page to allow time for the listener to turn the page.
- Label the tape and the tape container with the title and author of the book before returning it to school in a large Ziploc bag.

Supporting and extending the school curriculum

There are many ways that families can support their children's school experience through the connections with reading aloud. Many teachers find that the weekly or monthly newsletter that they send home is an excellent way to inform parents about what they can do to support what is happening at school. They suggest titles, authors, chapter books, and poetry books for parents to check out and read with their child. They also tell parents what the children are currently studying in science and social studies and suggest books on the topic for them to read with their children.

> I send a "reading log" home with the children each month. This log lists the titles and authors of the books we have read together as a class. I invite parents to look for these books at the library so they can reread them with their children. I find that not only does this facilitate parents reading to and with their child, it also lets the parents know what kinds of books we are reading in school. The reading log is a place for parents to start when trying to decide what to read with their child. The books may reinforce concepts we are studying or simply be enjoyable read-alouds.
>
> —*Emily*

> At the end of each month I sent home a list of all the books we had read aloud during the month. This list became a starting point for conversations about what was happening in school and about particular books that the children liked. Parents often tried to get favorites out of the library to read again to their children.
>
> —*Bobbi*

Follow-up projects

Some books lead to interesting at-home projects. Parents appreciate ideas for activities they can do with their children in connection with the books read at school. The projects and ideas are endless. For example, after reading *Thunder Cake* (Polacco) on a stormy school day, send the bibliographic information along with the real recipe for making the cake mentioned in the book.

> We read *Insects Are My Life* (McDonald), which tells the story of a girl who is crazy about bugs and insects. I suggested that parents and children go on an insect hunt together using a magnifying glass like the main character in the book, and that perhaps they could try to write down the names all of the insects that they saw.
>
> —Emily

Some suggestions are simple and don't require more than adding an item to the grocery list. For example, encourage parents to buy a peach for their child to try after reading *James and the Giant Peach* (Dahl). On baseball's opening day, read *How Georgie Radbourn Saved Baseball* (Shannon) to the class and send home a note suggesting parents play catch with their child.

Connecting with family experiences

We encourage parents to look for books on topics related to things going on in their family. These topics might be serious issues, like a death in the family, a new sibling, or a pending move. Families can also look for books that will connect children with everyday events in their lives. Is a family going to take a trip to the zoo? Perhaps they want to read about zoos and animals before or after the visit in *My Visit to the Zoo* (Aliki). If a member of the family is a police officer, read *Aero and Officer Mike: Police Partners* (Russell). Is the family expecting relatives from another state? Try to find both fiction (*The Relatives Came*, Rylant) and nonfiction (travel books) about where their visitors live.

Sending books home

Sending books home is one of the best ways to develop a lifelong love of reading and to keep the reading aloud habit going at home. It informs parents about the types of books being read at school, and it makes it easy for them to read with their child.

We encourage teachers to develop a system for children to take books home on a regular basis. Procedures vary, depending on the number of books available and on practical considerations about getting the books returned from home. Most teachers find that when they take the time in class to talk about how to take care of books and the importance of returning them within the agreed-upon time frame, children (and parents) respond positively.

If the books are part of your personal library, write your name on the inside and, if possible, with masking tape on the cover. On chapter books, you might put your name in large letters covering the outside pages. Sending books home in a plastic bag helps keep the books clean, makes them easier to find in a backpack, and signals to parents that it is a special book from school. Some teachers include an information sheet with selected books that includes other titles by the same author, other titles on the same subject or an idea for a family follow-up project.

> My "Borrow the Book" program works like a library. If a child wishes to borrow a book of mine, he or she fills out a borrowing form, which requires the child's name and the title and author of the book. I put the book in a Ziploc bag and then the child puts the book directly into his or her school bag. This ensures that the book actually goes home rather than gets "lost" in a desk, or left in a cubby or on the bus.
>
> I usually send borrowed books home on Mondays and we check them back in on Thursdays. I have found that having the books due Thursday helps get all of the books back to the class before the weekend. Those who forget to bring the book back on Thursday are reminded to bring it the next day. I allow children to borrow one book a week from my library, and they must return the book before borrowing another.
>
> —*Emily*

I developed different routines for checking out books, depending on the grade and time of year. One procedure involved writing on the chalkboard the names of children who were taking a book home. The next morning, they would show me the returned book and erase their name. I found that the easier the checkout procedure, the more books went home more often.

—Bobbi

The school library is also an important resource for books to go home. Most schools have a regular library period each week when children can check out a book. This experience helps them cultivate personal choices about the kinds of books they like while developing the habit of regular trips to the library. Whenever the library rules allow, we encourage children to go independently to the library throughout the week as they need a new book.

In my classroom we had a library book box where children could return their books if they brought them back before library day. This way there was a better chance that the books would not get lost among the other books in the room, and that the books would not be overdue on library day. Many children went independently during choice time.

—Bobbi

In summary, when parents ask what they can do to help their children in school, we suggest that they read to them every day. Although we explain the benefits of this daily practice, we always emphasize the most important one: reading aloud instills a lifetime love of reading as children learn to read.

Children's Works Cited

Ahlberg, Allan. 2000. *The Snail House*. Cambridge, MA: Candlewick Press.

Alborough, Jez. 1997. *Watch Out! Big Bro's Coming!* Cambridge, MA: Candlewick Press.

Aliki. 1997. *My Visit to the Zoo*. New York: HarperCollins.

Angelou, Maya. 1993. *Life Doesn't Frighten Me*. New York: Stewart, Tabori and Chang.

Arnold, Tedd. 1987. *The Signmaker's Assistant*. New York: Dial Books.

Arnold, Tedd. 1995. *No More Water in the Tub!* New York: Dial Books.

Brett, Jan. 1989. *The Mitten*. New York: G. P. Putnam's Sons.

Brett, Jan. 1992. *Trouble with Trolls*. New York: G. P. Putnam's Sons.

Brett, Jan. 1994. *Town Mouse Country Mouse*. New York: G. P. Putnam's Sons.

Brett, Jan. 1999. *Gingerbread Baby*. New York: G. P. Putnam's Sons.

Brown, Marc. 1987. *Arthur's Tooth*. New York: Joy Street Books.

Burton, Virginia Lee. 1943. *Katy and the Big Snow*. Boston: Houghton Mifflin.

Cannon, Janell. 1993. *Stellaluna*. New York: Harcourt Brace.

Carle, Eric. 1984. *The Very Busy Spider*. New York: Philomel.

Clement, Rod. 1991. *Counting on Frank*. Milwaukee, WI: Gareth Stevens.

Cole, Joanna. 1986. *The Magic School Bus at the Waterworks*. New York: Scholastic.

Cole, Joanna. 1992. *The Magic School Bus on the Ocean Floor.* New York: Scholastic.

Cole, Joanna. *The Magic School Bus* series of chapter books. New York: Scholastic.

Cosby, Bill. *Little Bill Books for Beginning Readers* series. New York: Scholastic.

Dahl, Roald. 1961. *James and the Giant Peach.* New York: Knopf.

d'Aulaire, Ingri. 1987. *Abe Lincoln.* Garden City, NY: Doubleday.

Davies, Nicola. 1997. *Big Blue Whale.* Cambridge, MA: Candlewick Press.

Day, Alexandra. 1989. *Carl Goes Shopping.* New York: Farrar, Straus & Giroux.

dePaola, Tomie. 1975. *Strega Nona.* New York: Simon & Schuster.

dePaola, Tomie. 1996. *The Baby Sister.* New York: G. P. Putnam's Sons.

Dotlich, Rebecca. 2001. *When Riddles Come Rumbling: Poems to Ponder.* Honesdale, PA: Boyds Mill Press.

Drew, David. 1990. *I Spy.* Crystal Lake, IL: Rigby.

Eastman, P. D. 1961. *Go Dog Go!* New York: Random House.

Fox, Mem. 1984. *Wilfred Gordon McDonald Partridge.* New York: Kane Miller.

Fox, Mem. 1988. *Koala Lou.* New York: Harcourt Brace Jovanovich.

Fox, Mem. 1994. *Time for Bed.* New York: Harcourt Brace Jovanovich.

Fox, Mem. 1995. *Tough Boris.* New York: Harcourt Brace.

Freeman, Don. 1978. *A Pocket for Corduroy.* New York: Viking Press.

Garland, Michael. 1998. *Angel Cat.* Honesdale, PA: Boyds Mills Press.

Giff, Patricia Reilly. *The Kids of the Polk Street School* series. New York: Yearling Books.

Goldstein, Bobbye S. 1992. *Inner Chimes: Poems on Poetry.* Honesdale, PA: Boyds Mills Press.

Goodman, Joan Elizabeth. 2001. *Bernard Goes to School.* Honesdale, PA: Boyds Mills Press.

Harley, Avis. 2001. *Leap into Poetry: More ABCs of Poetry.* Honesdale, PA: Boyds Mills Press.

Harrison, David. 2002. *Rivers: Nature's Wondrous Waterways.* Honesdale, PA: Boyds Mills Press.

Harness, Cheryl. 1997. *Abe Lincoln Goes to Washington, 1837–1865.* New York: Scholastic.

Heller, Ruth. 1987. *A Cache of Jewels and Other Collective Nouns.* New York: Grosset & Dunlap.

Henkes, Kevin. 1991. *Chrysanthemum.* New York: Greenwillow.

Henkes, Kevin. 1996. *Lilly's Purple Plastic Purse.* New York: Greenwillow.

Hobbie, Holly. 1998. *Toot and Puddle: A Present for Toot.* Boston: Little, Brown.

Holbrook, Sara. 2002. *Wham! It's a Poetry Jam: Discovering Performance in Poetry.* Honesdale, PA: Boyds Mills Press.

Hopkins, Lee Bennett. 1997. *Marvelous Math: A Book of Poems.* New York: Scholastic.

Howker, Janni. 1997. *Walk with a Wolf.* Cambridge, MA: Candlewick Press.

Igus, Toyomi. 1998. *I See the Rhythm.* San Francisco: Children's Book Press.

James, Betsy. 1999. *Tadpoles.* New York: Dutton Children's Books.

Janeczko, Paul. 2001. *A Poke in the I: A Collection of Concrete Poems.* Cambridge, MA: Candlewick Press.

Jenkins, Martin. 1996. *Fly Traps! Plants That Bite Back.* Cambridge, MA: Candlewick Press.

Johnston, Tony. 1996. *Once in the Country: Poems of a Farm.* New York: G. P. Putnam's Sons.

Keats, Ezra Jack. 1962. *The Snowy Day.* New York: Viking Press.

Kellogg, Steven. 2000. *The Missing Mitten Mystery.* New York: Dial Books.

Laminack, Lester. 1998. *Trevor's Wiggly-Wobbly Tooth.* Atlanta: Peachtree Publishers.

Leedy, Loreen. 1997. *Measuring Penny.* New York: Henry Holt.

Leedy, Loreen. 2000. *Mapping Penny's World*. New York: Henry Holt.

Llewellyn, Claire. 1996. *Disguises and Surprises*. Cambridge, MA: Candlewick Press.

Longfellow, Henry Wadsworth. 2001. *The Midnight Ride of Paul Revere*. New York: Handprint Books.

Macaulay, David. 1975. *Pyramid*. Boston: Houghton Mifflin.

Martin, Bill, Jr. 1987. *Brown Bear, Brown Bear, What Do You See?* New York: Henry Holt.

Martin, Bill, Jr., and John Archambault. 1989. *Chicka-Chicka-Boom-Boom*. New York: Simon & Schuster.

Martin, Rafe. 1993. *The Boy Who Lived with the Seals*. New York: G. P. Putnam's Sons.

McCloskey, Robert. 1941. *Make Way for Ducklings*. New York: Viking Press.

McCloskey, Robert. 1948. *Blueberries for Sal*. New York: Viking Press.

McDermott, Gerald. 1974. *Arrow to the Sun*. New York: Viking Press.

McDonald, Megan. 1995. *Insects Are My Life*. New York: Orchard Books.

Moss, Lloyd. 1995. *Zin! Zin! Zin! a Violin*. New York: Simon & Schuster.

Murphy, Stuart J. *MathStart* series. New York: HarperCollins.

Murrow, Liza K. 1989. *Good-bye, Sammy*. New York: Holiday House.

Olaleye, Isacc. 1998. *Lake of the Big Snake*. Honesdale, PA: Boyds Mills Press.

Osborne, Mary Pope. *Magic Tree House* books. New York: Random House.

Park, Barbara. *Junie B. Jones* series. New York: Random House.

Parkes, Brenda. 1990. *The Royal Dinner*. Hawthorn, Australia: Mimosa Publications.

Perry, Sarah. 1995. *If . . .* Venice, CA: Children's Library Press.

Piper, Watty. 1961. *The Little Engine That Could*. New York: Platt and Munk.

Pinkney, Andrea Davis. 1998. *Duke Ellington*. New York: Hyperion.

Polacco, Patricia. 1990. *Thunder Cake*. New York: Philomel.

Polacco, Patricia. 1994. *My Rotten Red-Headed Older Brother*. New York: Philomel.

Polacco, Patricia. 1996. *Aunt Chip and the Great Triple Creek Dam Affair*. New York: Philomel.

Preller, James. *Jigsaw Jones Mysteries*. New York: Scholastic.

Priceman, Marjorie. 1994. *How to Make an Apple Pie and See the World*. New York: Knopf.

Rappaport, Doreen. 2002. *No More! Stories and Songs of Slave Resistance*. Cambridge, MA: Candlewick Press.

Russell, Joan Plummer. 2001. *Aero and Officer Mike: Police Partners*. Honesdale, PA: Boyds Mills Press.

Rylant, Cynthia. 1986. *The Relatives Came*. New York: Random House.

Rylant, Cynthia. *The Cobble Street Cousins* series. New York: Simon & Schuster.

Rylant, Cynthia. *Henry and Mudge* series. New York: Aladdin Paperbacks.

Sabuda, Robert. 1994. *Tutankhamen's Gift*. New York: Atheneum.

Scieszka, Jon. 1989. *The True Story of the 3 Little Pigs by A. Wolf*. New York: Viking.

Scieszka, Jon. 1995. *Math Curse*. New York: Viking.

Sendak, Maurice. 1963. *Where the Wild Things Are*. New York: Scholastic.

Shannon, David. 1994. *How Georgie Radbourn Saved Baseball*. New York: Scholastic.

Sharmat, Marjorie Weinman. *Nate the Great* books. New York: Yearling.

Slate, Joseph. 1996. *Miss Bindergarten Gets Ready for Kindergarten*. New York: Dutton Children's Books.

Slate, Joseph. 1998. *Miss Bindergarten Celebrates the 100th Day of Kindergarten*. New York: Dutton Children's Books.

Slate, Joseph. 2000. *Miss Bindergarten Stays Home from Kindergarten*. New York: Dutton Children's Books.

Slate, Joseph. 2001. *Miss Bindergarten Takes a Field Trip with Kindergarten*. New York: Dutton Children's Books.

Stevenson, Robert Louis. 1990. *My Shadow*. New York: G. P. Putnam's Sons.

Stoeke, Janet Morgan. 1986. *Minerva Louise at School*. New York: Dutton Children's Books

Thayer, Ernest. L. 1987. *Casey at the Bat*. New York: Workman.

Trivizas, Eugene. 1993. *The Three Little Wolves and the Big Bad Pig*. New York: Aladdin Paperbacks.

Viorst, Judith. 1972. *Alexander and the Terrible, Horrible, No Good, Very Bad Day*. New York: Atheneum.

Viorst, Judith. 1976. *The Tenth Good Thing About Barney*. New York: Simon & Schuster.

Viorst, Judith. 1978. *Alexander, Who Used to Be Rich Last Sunday*. New York: Atheneum.

Viorst, Judith. 1995. *Alexander, Who's Not (Do You Hear Me? I Mean It!) Going to Move*. New York: Simon & Schuster.

Walsh, Ellen Stoll. 1989. *Mouse Paint*. New York: Harcourt.

Walsh, Jill. 1994. *Pepi and the Secret Names*. New York: Lothrop, Lee & Shepard.

Warner, Gertrude Chandler. *The Boxcar Children* series. New York: Albert Whitman.

Weatherford, Carole Boston. 2000. *The Sound That Jazz Makes*. New York: Walker and Company.

References

Barrs, Myra, and Sue Ellis. 1998. *Reading Together Parents' Handbook.* Cambridge, MA: Candlewick Press.

Fisher, Bobbi. 1995. *Thinking and Learning Together: Curriculum and Community in a Primary Classroom.* Portsmouth, NH: Heinemann.

Fisher, Bobbi. 1997. *Classroom Close-ups: Bobbi Fisher: Organization and Management; Developing Young Readers; Guiding Young Authors.* Bothell, WA: Wright Group. Videotape.

Fisher, Bobbi. 1998. *Joyful Learning in Kindergarten.* Portsmouth, NH: Heinemann.

Fisher, Bobbi, and Emily Fisher Medvic. 2000. *Perspectives on Shared Reading.* Portsmouth, NH: Heinemann.

Fox, Mem. 2001. *Reading Magic.* New York: Harcourt.

Holdaway, Don. 1979. *Foundations of Literacy.* Portsmouth, NH: Heinemann.

Trelease, Jim. 2001. *The New Read-Aloud Handbook.* 5th ed. New York: Penguin.